Prowl and Thrive

Prowl and Thrive

Matthew Petchinsky

Prowl and Thrive: The Lion's Guide to Success
By: Matthew Petchinsky

Introduction

The Lion's Path to Power, Purpose, and Prosperity

In the heart of the savannah, the lion reigns supreme. With its powerful stride, commanding presence, and unwavering confidence, the lion embodies what it means to be a leader, a warrior, and a survivor. It does not simply exist—it prowls, strategizes, dominates, and thrives. *Prowl and Thrive: The Lion's Guide to Success* is more than just a book; it is a philosophy, a blueprint for those who dare to embrace their inner lion and unleash their full potential in every aspect of life.

In the wild, survival is not guaranteed. It is not given. It is earned through intelligence, action, and resilience. The same is true in the modern world—whether in business, personal growth, relationships, or financial prosperity. To thrive, you must embody the qualities of a lion: strength, adaptability, fearlessness, and an unshakable belief in your own power. This book is your guide to stepping into that power, taking control of your destiny, and ruling over your own domain.

Why the Lion?

The lion is not the largest, fastest, or even the strongest animal in the wild—yet it is the king. Why? Because the lion possesses an undeniable mindset of dominance. Unlike the gazelle that flees at the first sign of danger or the hyena that scavenges off the work of others, the lion *seizes* opportunities, *hunts* with precision, and *thrives* under pressure.

Success in life is not reserved for those who wait, hesitate, or play it safe. It belongs to those who act boldly, plan wisely, and move with confidence. The lion teaches us that success is a combination of courage, strategic action, and the ability to recognize opportunities even in the face of challenges.

In this book, we will explore the **"Lion's Code"—a set of principles that will transform the way you think, act, and succeed.** You will learn how to prowl through life with calculated moves, thrive in the face of adversity, and command the respect you deserve.

The Prowl and Thrive Mindset

Many people live life passively. They wait for opportunities to come, hope that luck will favor them, and play it safe in fear of failure. But the lion does not wait—it **creates its own opportunities**. It hunts. It dominates. It thrives.

If you are tired of merely existing and are ready to take control of your life, then this book will teach you how to:

- **Develop the mindset of a lion** – One that is fearless, decisive, and powerful.
- **Hunt for success relentlessly** – Learn how to set goals, strategize, and execute with precision.
- **Roar with confidence** – Build unshakable self-belief and command respect in every area of your life.
- **Defend your territory** – Create an empire of wealth, personal power, and independence.
- **Thrive in adversity** – Learn to embrace challenges, failures, and obstacles as fuel for growth.

Who Is This Book For?

This book is for the **bold, the ambitious, and the unstoppable**. It is for the **entrepreneur** who wants to build a thriving business, the **leader** who wants to command respect, the **visionary** who wants to turn ideas into reality, and the **individual** who refuses to settle for mediocrity.

It is for those who are tired of playing small, making excuses, and waiting for life to change. This book will show you how to take **radical control of your life, your success, and your destiny.**

How to Use This Book

Prowl and Thrive is not just another self-help book. It is a **battle manual**, a **mindset reset**, and a **strategic playbook** for success. Each chapter is designed to give you actionable insights that you can implement immediately.

- Read **each chapter with the mindset of a hunter**—absorb the knowledge and apply it.
- Take **notes, reflect, and strategize**—this book is meant to challenge you to think and act differently.
- Put **principles into action**—success is not about what you know, but what you *do*.

At the end of this journey, you will have transformed from someone who merely *exists* into someone who prowls with purpose, hunts with precision, and thrives in every aspect of life.

It's Time to Roar

The world is full of followers, but the throne belongs to those who dare to lead. You are not a bystander in your own story. You are the lion. You are the hunter. You are the ruler of your destiny.

So step forward, claim your power, and let the world hear your roar. Let's begin.

Chapter 1: Understanding the Terrain
Mastering the Environment to Maximize Your Success

Success is not random. It is not luck. It is not a fluke. It is a result of those who understand the terrain they move through, recognize the obstacles ahead, and strategically position themselves to overcome challenges and seize opportunities.

Just like a lion must understand its environment—where the prey moves, where the dangers lurk, and where the best hunting grounds are—you must learn to read the landscape of your own life, business, and ambitions. Whether you're looking to dominate in your career, build financial wealth, or achieve personal growth, your ability to assess and adapt to your surroundings will determine how effectively you prowl and thrive.

The Law of the Jungle: Why Your Environment Matters

The lion does not waste energy hunting where there is no prey. It does not fight battles it cannot win. It does not hesitate when an opportunity presents itself. Why? Because it understands its environment.

In the modern world, **your terrain is your industry, your financial landscape, your relationships, your network, your personal strengths and weaknesses, and the competitive forces around you.**

If you do not understand the environment you operate in, you will become prey instead of a predator. You will wander aimlessly, hoping for success rather than designing it.

Your Personal Terrain: Identifying Your Strengths and Weaknesses

Every lion has its own advantages. Some are more powerful, others are faster, and some are better hunters. The key is understanding what *your* unique strengths are and how to leverage them to succeed.

Ask yourself:

- **What are my natural strengths?**
  - Are you highly analytical? Creative? A natural leader? A great communicator?
- **What are my weaknesses?**
  - Do you struggle with discipline? Do you avoid conflict? Do you procrastinate?
- **What environments bring out the best in me?**
  - Do you thrive in competitive spaces? Do you do better in structured routines or creative freedom?

By identifying your strengths, you can sharpen them into powerful tools. By acknowledging your weaknesses, you can mitigate them before they become obstacles.

Your External Terrain: The Industry and Competitive Landscape

The lion does not hunt the same way in the dry season as it does in the rainy season. It adapts based on the conditions of its environment.

Similarly, success in the modern world requires you to be highly aware of the industry you're in, the trends shaping it, and the competitors sharing your space.

To dominate your terrain, you must:

- Study the **key players** in your industry. Who is leading? What makes them successful?
- Recognize the **shifting trends**. What changes are happening? What opportunities are emerging?
- Identify the **gaps and weaknesses** in your field. Where can you provide value that others have missed?

Many people fail simply because they enter an environment blindly. They start businesses without studying the market, launch products without knowing their audience, or try to become leaders without understanding the expectations of their followers.

To prowl and thrive, you must be intentional about where you step and how you move.

The Terrain of Opportunity: Recognizing When to Strike

A lion does not waste energy chasing weak opportunities. It stalks, observes, and waits for the perfect moment to strike.

In life, many people chase every idea, every project, every trend—wasting time, energy, and resources on things that do not serve them. The key to success is **selectivity**.

Before committing to an opportunity, ask yourself:

- **Is this aligned with my strengths and long-term goals?**
- **Does this opportunity have real growth potential, or is it a short-term distraction?**
- **Am I in the right position to execute effectively, or do I need to sharpen my skills first?**

Success comes to those who pick their battles wisely.

The Terrain of Danger: Recognizing Threats Before They Strike

Even the strongest lions can be brought down by hidden dangers—poachers, rival predators, or environmental changes. The same applies to your journey.

Many people fail not because they lack talent, but because they fail to recognize the dangers ahead.

Common threats include:

- **Toxic environments** – Being surrounded by negativity, doubt, or people who do not believe in your potential.
- **Lack of preparation** – Entering new ventures without the necessary knowledge or strategy.
- **Distractions and comfort zones** – Losing focus due to comfort or chasing unnecessary pleasures instead of real progress.
- **Fear and self-doubt** – Letting imposter syndrome or hesitation stop you from taking action.

To thrive, you must be as aware of the threats in your environment as you are of the opportunities. The lion is never reckless—it is calculated, patient, and decisive.

Adapting to Changing Terrain: The Power of Flexibility

A lion that refuses to adapt dies. If water sources dry up, it moves. If prey migrates, it follows. **Success is about adaptability.**

Many people fail because they refuse to evolve. They cling to old habits, outdated skills, or dying industries, hoping things will stay the same.

If you want to dominate your environment, you must:

- **Stay informed** – Keep learning about new developments in your industry.
- **Be flexible** – When things change, adjust your approach instead of resisting.
- **Expand your skill set** – Keep growing so you can survive in any condition.

Those who thrive are those who are willing to shift, pivot, and evolve when necessary.

Conclusion: Prowl with Awareness, Thrive with Mastery

The lion does not rule the savannah by accident. It rules because it **understands its terrain** better than any other predator. It knows where to hunt, when to strike, and how to navigate challenges.

You must do the same.

By mastering your personal landscape—your strengths, weaknesses, industry, opportunities, and threats—you position yourself to **not only survive but thrive**. The path ahead is not random; it is determined by how well you read, understand, and dominate your environment.

Chapter 2: Building Your Personal Strategy
Crafting Your Blueprint for Unstoppable Success

A lion does not hunt blindly. It does not waste energy chasing prey without a plan. It stalks, observes, calculates, and then executes with precision. Every movement is strategic. Every step is intentional.

Success in life and business operates on the same principle. Without a clear **personal strategy**, you will wander aimlessly, chasing opportunities that do not serve you, reacting to life instead of shaping it. *Building Your Personal Strategy* is about crafting a clear and actionable plan that aligns with your goals, strengths, and environment—allowing you to prowl with confidence and thrive with certainty.

This chapter will guide you through the process of **developing a powerful, lion-like strategy** that ensures every action you take moves you closer to your ultimate vision.

The Power of a Strategic Mindset

Most people operate reactively. They respond to circumstances instead of creating them. **But lions do not react—they anticipate, plan, and dominate.**

To succeed at anything—whether it's building wealth, starting a business, mastering a skill, or achieving personal growth—you must develop a strategic mindset. This means:

- Thinking long-term while executing short-term.
- Making decisions based on calculated moves, not emotions.
- Understanding the difference between **hunting (proactive action)** and **scavenging (reactive survival).**

A strategic mind is one that is always **five moves ahead**, considering the risks, rewards, and consequences of every decision before taking action.

Step 1: Defining Your Ultimate Goal (Your Lion's Vision)

Every lion has a purpose—survival, dominance, and legacy. What is yours?

Before building a strategy, you must first establish a **clear, powerful goal** that excites and challenges you. This is your *Lion's Vision*—the destination that fuels your hunger for success.

How to Set a Powerful Goal:

1. **Make it specific.**
   - Instead of saying *"I want to be successful,"* say *"I want to build a six-figure business in 12 months."*
2. **Make it measurable.**
   - Can you track your progress? Define milestones that show you're moving forward.
3. **Make it time-bound.**
   - A lion does not hunt forever; it has a window of opportunity. Set a deadline for achieving your goal.
4. **Make it meaningful.**
   - Does your goal excite you? Does it challenge you? If your goal doesn't light a fire in you, it's not strong enough.

◈ **Lion's Exercise:** Write down the **one** goal that would change your life the most if you achieved it in the next 12 months.

Step 2: Understanding Your Current Position (The Lion's Self-Assessment)

You cannot build a strategy without first knowing where you stand. Just as a lion surveys its surroundings before making a move, you must take stock of your current strengths, weaknesses, resources, and obstacles.

Ask Yourself:

- **What are my greatest strengths?**
    - What skills, talents, or experiences make me powerful?
- **What weaknesses or gaps must I improve?**
    - Where do I lack knowledge, discipline, or resources?
- **What threats or obstacles are in my way?**
    - Competition? Financial struggles? A lack of motivation?
- **What resources and allies do I have?**
    - Who and what can help me achieve my goals faster?

◈ **Lion's Exercise:** Write down **three strengths** you can leverage and **three weaknesses** you must improve to reach your goal.

Step 3: Crafting Your Battle Plan (The Lion's Roadmap)

A lion does not wake up and wander the savannah hoping to stumble upon food. It follows a structured plan, moving from one target to the next. Your strategy must work the same way.

Break Your Goal into Tactical Steps:

Instead of treating success as one giant, intimidating task, break it down into **actionable steps** that move you forward each day.

1. **Quarterly Objectives:**
   - What must you achieve in the next 3 months to move closer to your goal?
2. **Monthly Milestones:**
   - What must be completed each month?
3. **Weekly Action Steps:**
   - What tasks will you focus on each week?
4. **Daily Execution:**
   - What actions must you take every single day?

◇ *Example Strategy for a Business Owner:*

- **Goal:** Build a six-figure online store in 12 months.
- **Quarter 1:** Research market, build website, test products.
- **Quarter 2:** Launch marketing campaigns, drive sales.
- **Quarter 3:** Optimize, scale, automate.
- **Quarter 4:** Expand to new markets, establish brand dominance.

◇ **Lion's Exercise:** Break your main goal into **4 quarterly objectives**, then outline **monthly and weekly action steps**.

Step 4: The Power of Adaptability (Pivot Like a Predator)

No hunt ever goes perfectly. Sometimes the prey moves unexpectedly. Sometimes conditions change.

A lion adapts, but never loses focus.

As you work toward your goal, you must be willing to adjust your strategy when necessary. This does NOT mean abandoning your vision—it means adjusting your tactics when obstacles arise.

Signs It's Time to Pivot:

- **If you hit a dead end:** The method isn't working, and you need a new approach.
- **If the terrain shifts:** Market trends, opportunities, or challenges change.
- **If you find a better path:** You discover a smarter, faster way to achieve success.

◈ **Lion's Exercise:** Write down **one potential challenge** that could slow down your progress and a plan for how you will adapt.

Step 5: Building Relentless Discipline (Hunting Until You Succeed)

A lion does not give up after one failed hunt. It **persists**. It **learns**. It **improves**.

The difference between winners and losers is **discipline**—the ability to stay committed even when motivation fades.

How to Build Unstoppable Discipline:

1. **Create a ritual of execution.**
   - Set a fixed schedule for working toward your goal every single day.
2. **Hold yourself accountable.**
   - Track progress weekly. If you're off course, adjust immediately.
3. **Cut out distractions.**
   - Eliminate habits and environments that slow you down.
4. **Surround yourself with winners.**
   - Join networks, mentors, or communities that push you forward.

◇ **Lion's Exercise:** Identify **one habit** you must remove and **one discipline** you must develop to stay focused on your goal.

Conclusion: Move with Strategy, Dominate with Precision

A lion does not leave its success to chance. It operates with a **clear plan, unwavering focus, and unrelenting persistence.**

If you follow the **Lion's Strategy**, you will no longer be aimless. You will no longer hope for success. You will be in **control, moving with power**, and **executing with precision.**

Your Success Blueprint Recap:

⬥ Define your **Lion's Vision** (your main goal).

⬥ Assess your **current strengths, weaknesses, and resources**.

⬥ Build a **battle plan** with clear milestones.

⬥ **Adapt like a predator** when obstacles arise.

⬥ Develop **unbreakable discipline** to keep hunting until you win.

The world belongs to those who **prowl with strategy and strike with confidence.**

Are you ready to move like a lion? Then let's continue.

Chapter 3: Thriving Amidst Competition
Outmaneuver, Outlast, and Outshine the Rest

In the wild, every lion faces competition. Rival predators lurk, challengers seek dominance, and survival is never guaranteed. The same holds true in life—whether in business, personal development, or career advancement, competition is inevitable. The question is not **if** you will face competitors but **how** you will rise above them.

A lion does not shrink in the presence of rivals. It asserts its dominance. It stands its ground. It strategizes, fights, and claims victory. *Thriving Amidst Competition* is about learning how to **not just survive but to dominate**, ensuring that no one can take what rightfully belongs to you.

The Competitive Mindset: Thinking Like a Lion

The most successful people do not fear competition—they **welcome it**. They understand that challenges force growth, push boundaries, and sharpen their instincts. To thrive, you must:

- **Stop seeing competition as a threat** and start seeing it as fuel.
- **Refuse to play small** or let fear hold you back.
- **Become a strategic competitor** who anticipates moves before they happen.

Lions thrive not because they are the strongest, but because they are the most strategic and fearless hunters in the wild.

Step 1: Identifying Your Competitors

Every lion knows its rivals—their strengths, weaknesses, and patterns. You must do the same. **If you don't know who your competition is, you are already at a disadvantage.**

Who Are Your Competitors?

Competitors are not just businesses or individuals in your industry—they are **anything that stands between you and your success.** This can include:

- **Direct competitors** – People or businesses offering the same product, service, or skill as you.
- **Indirect competitors** – Alternatives that solve the same problem in a different way.
- **Internal competition** – Your own doubts, fears, and bad habits.

◈ **Lion's Exercise:** Identify **three major competitors** in your space. Analyze what makes them successful and where they are vulnerable.

Step 2: Differentiation – The Art of Standing Out

A lion does not compete by being just another predator—it **commands presence and dominates its space**. To thrive, you must separate yourself from the pack.

How to Stand Out from the Competition

1. **Unique Strengths:**
   - What do you do better than anyone else?
   - What special skills, insights, or approaches do you bring?
2. **Branding and Positioning:**
   - Are you seen as a leader in your space?
   - Do people associate your name with excellence?
3. **Innovation and Creativity:**
   - Are you constantly evolving and improving?
   - Do you introduce fresh ideas instead of copying others?
4. **Unbreakable Confidence:**
   - Do you project authority and certainty in everything you do?
   - Confidence alone can make you an unstoppable force.

◇ **Lion's Exercise:** Write down **one powerful way you can stand out from your competitors** starting today.

Step 3: The Power of Aggressive Strategy

Lions do not wait for opportunities—they **seize them**. They are aggressive when needed, patient when necessary, and always thinking two steps ahead.

Winning Competitive Strategies

- **Be Faster:** Execute before your competitors. Speed creates an advantage.
- **Be Smarter:** Study their weaknesses and use them to your benefit.
- **Be More Persistent:** Many competitors give up when things get tough—outlast them.
- **Be More Adaptable:** When conditions change, adjust your approach instantly.

◇ **Lion's Exercise:** Identify one aggressive move you can make this week to get ahead of your competition.

Step 4: The Role of Territory – Defending What's Yours

Lions establish territories and **do not allow invaders to take over their domain**. Whether it's your business, reputation, or market position, you must do the same.

How to Protect Your Space:

1. **Become the Best in Your Niche:**
   ◦ Master your craft so that people recognize your authority.
   ◦ Deliver **undeniable** value that keeps people coming to you.
2. **Build a Loyal Following:**
   ◦ Engage with your audience, customers, or supporters consistently.
   ◦ Establish a **deep connection** that keeps them loyal to you, not your competitors.
3. **Control Your Narrative:**
   ◦ Never let competitors define your reputation—**own your story**.
   ◦ Stay active in your industry, network, or community so your name remains **respected** and **dominant**.

◈ **Lion's Exercise:** What steps can you take to build a stronger reputation or following? List three things you can implement now.

Step 5: Turning Competition Into an Advantage

A lion does not fear competition because it understands **one truth**—competition forces it to **evolve, improve, and stay sharp**. The presence of rivals pushes you to be better than you were yesterday.

How to Use Competition as Fuel for Growth

- **Observe and Learn:**
    - What are your competitors doing right? Adapt and improve upon it.
- **Outwork Them:**
    - Most people won't put in the extra effort—do what they won't.
- **Control the Energy You Give Them:**
    - Do not waste energy worrying about competitors—**stay focused on your own mission**.

◇ **Lion's Exercise:** Identify **one lesson** you've learned from a competitor and **how you can apply it to improve your own strategy.**

Step 6: Winning the Long Game – Sustaining Your Dominance

Thriving in competition is not about quick victories—it's about **long-term dominance**. Many people get ahead temporarily but fail because they cannot sustain success.

The Secrets to Long-Term Success:

◇ **Never get comfortable.** Keep evolving, growing, and adapting.

◇ **Surround yourself with winners.** Stay connected to ambitious, high-level thinkers.

◇ **Stay consistent.** Small daily actions lead to massive long-term success.

◇ **Be relentless.** Lions never stop hunting—they only sharpen their skills.

◇ **Lion's Exercise:** Write down a long-term strategy that will ensure your continued growth and dominance over the next year.

Conclusion: The Lion's Competitive Edge

Competition is not your enemy. **It is your sharpening stone.** It is what forces you to grow, adapt, and become an unstoppable force.

By implementing the strategies in this chapter, you will not only **survive the competition—you will dominate it.**

Your Competitive Advantage Recap:

◇ Identify your **competition** and analyze their strengths/weaknesses.

◇ **Differentiate** yourself by standing out in a unique and powerful way.

◇ Develop an **aggressive strategy** to stay ahead.

◇ **Defend your territory** and build an unshakable reputation.

◇ **Use competition as a tool** for growth instead of fearing it.

◇ **Play the long game**—consistency and evolution ensure lasting dominance.

The lion does not wait for permission to succeed—it **takes what it deserves.**

Are you ready to rise above the rest? Then let's move forward.

Chapter 4: Staying Focused on the Goal
The Lion's Unwavering Determination to Thrive

A lion does not chase every animal it sees. It does not waste its energy on distractions. It sets its sights on its target, stalks with precision, and strikes with absolute focus. In the same way, your ability to **stay focused on your goal** is the difference between achieving massive success and wandering aimlessly.

The modern world is full of distractions—social media, unnecessary obligations, self-doubt, and a thousand voices pulling you in different directions. **If you lack focus, you will lose sight of your path.** You will start chasing things that do not serve you, wasting energy on goals that do not align with your vision.

To thrive like a lion, you must cultivate **ruthless focus, eliminate distractions, and keep moving forward, no matter the obstacles in your way.** This chapter will equip you with the tools to sharpen your focus and ensure that nothing pulls you away from your purpose.

Step 1: The Power of a Singular Vision

A lion does not hunt multiple animals at once. It picks one, stalks it, and ensures success before moving to the next.

Many people fail because they spread themselves too thin, attempting to chase **too many goals at once.** Success does not come from doing *everything*—it comes from doing **one thing with mastery and intensity.**

How to Define and Lock in Your Primary Goal

1. **Clarify Your Goal** – What is the ONE thing you must achieve in the next year that will change everything for you?
2. **Make It Specific and Measurable** – General goals (e.g., "I want to be rich") lack power. Instead, say: "I want to generate $100,000 in revenue in 12 months."

3. **Write It Down and Look at It Daily** – Studies show that people who write down their goals are significantly more likely to achieve them.

◇ **Lion's Exercise:** Write your main goal for the next 12 months and place it somewhere you will see it every day.

Step 2: Eliminating Distractions Like a Predator

In the wild, a distracted lion is a dead lion. If it loses focus, it fails the hunt. If it hesitates, another predator takes over.

Distractions are your **greatest enemy**. If you allow them, they will steal your time, drain your energy, and leave you frustrated, wondering why you are not making progress.

Common Distractions That Kill Focus and How to Eliminate Them

1. **Social Media & Digital Overload**
   - Solution: Set strict time limits for social media and remove notifications.
2. **Too Many Commitments**
   - Solution: Learn to say NO to things that do not serve your mission.
3. **Lack of Clear Priorities**
   - Solution: Use a **daily focus list** (limit yourself to 3 major tasks per day).
4. **Negative Influences**
   - Solution: Surround yourself with people who push you forward, not pull you down.
5. **Self-Doubt and Mental Clutter**
   - Solution: Remind yourself daily why your goal matters. Develop affirmations and a winning mindset.

◇ **Lion's Exercise:** Identify **three distractions** holding you back and make a plan to eliminate them today.

Step 3: The Art of Relentless Discipline

A lion does not wait to "feel motivated" before hunting. It moves **because it must**—because survival depends on it.

Motivation is **temporary**. Discipline is **permanent**. If you rely on motivation, you will only take action when you feel like it. But if you build discipline, you will take action **no matter what**.

How to Build Ruthless Discipline

◇ **Create a daily ritual** – Success comes from habits, not random effort. Establish a structured routine that guarantees progress.

◇ **Master self-control** – Avoid impulsive actions that do not align with your goals.

◇ **Push through resistance** – The best opportunities exist **just beyond your comfort zone.**

◇ **Develop unshakable patience** – Lions do not rush the hunt. They wait for the right moment.

◇ **Lion's Exercise:** Create a **daily success ritual**—a set of 3-5 things you will do every single day to move toward your goal.

Step 4: Overcoming Obstacles Without Losing Focus

Every lion faces resistance. The prey runs. The rival predators attack. The harsh elements make the hunt difficult. But the lion does not stop. It **adapts, pushes forward, and succeeds despite the challenge.**

Many people lose focus **when things get hard.** They encounter obstacles and start doubting their path.

How to Overcome Challenges Without Losing Momentum

- **View obstacles as part of the process** – Expect challenges and see them as a test of your strength.
- **Stay adaptable** – If one approach does not work, find another route.
- **Use failures as learning tools** – Every mistake contains a lesson that sharpens you.
- **Refuse to retreat** – Once you commit to a goal, you **must** see it through.

⬦ **Lion's Exercise:** Think of the **biggest obstacle** you are currently facing. Write down three solutions and take action on one today.

Step 5: The Focus-Driven Daily System

A lion does not waste time. Every move is calculated. You must structure your days with the same intensity.

The Ultimate Focus Formula: The Lion's Daily Structure

1. **Morning: Set the Tone for the Day**
   - Review your main goal.
   - Plan your top 3 priorities.
   - Eliminate early distractions.
2. **Midday: Execute With Relentless Precision**
   - Block out focused work time (no interruptions).
   - Track progress on tasks.
3. **Evening: Review and Reset**
   - Assess what worked and what needs adjustment.
   - Plan for tomorrow.

◈ **Lion's Exercise:** Design your **ideal daily routine** that prioritizes focus, execution, and self-improvement.

Step 6: The Mental Fortress – Developing Unbreakable Focus

A lion does not allow fear, doubt, or external pressures to dictate its actions. It **trusts itself completely.**

To master focus, you must build a **mental fortress** that protects your mind from distractions, negativity, and hesitation.

How to Build an Indestructible Mindset

1. **Control Your Inner Dialogue** – Replace doubts with affirmations.
2. **Visualize Your Success Daily** – See yourself achieving your goal.
3. **Limit Exposure to Negative People** – Surround yourself with driven, focused individuals.
4. **Commit Fully** – A half-hearted lion never wins the hunt. Go **all in** on your goal.

◈ **Lion's Exercise:** Create **a personal mantra** that reinforces your focus. Repeat it every morning and night.

Conclusion: Dominate with Relentless Focus

Distractions are the enemy of success. **A lion never loses focus on its prey. It does not waste energy on what does not serve it.**

To thrive, you must **lock in your vision, eliminate distractions, build discipline, overcome obstacles, and execute daily with absolute intensity.**

Your Focus Mastery Recap:

◈ Define **ONE primary goal** and commit to it.

◈ Eliminate **all distractions** that steal your time and energy.

◈ Build **unbreakable discipline**—work whether you feel like it or not.

◈ Face **challenges head-on** and push forward no matter what.

◈ Create a **daily system** that maximizes execution.

◈ Build a **mental fortress** that keeps you focused and unstoppable.

Success belongs to those who **prowl with purpose and never lose sight of their hunt.**

Chapter 5: Harnessing Inner Strength

Unleashing the Power Within to Dominate Your Journey

A lion's true strength does not come from its claws or its roar—it comes from within. It is the unshakable confidence in its own power, the relentless will to survive, and the unwavering belief that it belongs at the top of the food chain. **This is inner strength.**

In life, external success—money, status, achievements—is meaningless without inner strength. You may encounter obstacles, setbacks, and fierce competition, but if your **inner core is strong**, nothing can break you. When you **harness your inner strength**, you become an unstoppable force, moving through life with the power and presence of a lion.

This chapter will guide you in **discovering, developing, and harnessing your inner strength** to ensure that no challenge, failure, or fear can stand in your way.

Step 1: Understanding Inner Strength – The Core of a Lion

Lions are not born kings—they become kings through battles, survival, and the mastery of their instincts.

Inner strength is not about arrogance or brute force. It is about **having an unbreakable core that allows you to remain steady and powerful, no matter what life throws at you.**

The Four Pillars of Inner Strength

1. **Unshakable Self-Belief** Trusting yourself even when no one else does.
2. **Mental Resilience** – Bouncing back stronger from failures and setbacks.
3. **Emotional Mastery** – Controlling your emotions instead of being controlled by them.
4. **Relentless Determination** – Never quitting, no matter how hard the journey gets.

◈ **Lion's Exercise:** Rate yourself from 1-10 on each of the four pillars above. Identify which area needs the most improvement.

Step 2: Cultivating Unshakable Self-Belief

A lion does not need permission to be great—it **knows** it is great. **It does not seek approval from weaker creatures.**

The most successful people share this trait: **they believe in themselves even when no one else does.**

How to Build Unshakable Self-Belief

◇ **Own Your Power** – Stop playing small to make others comfortable.

◇ **Challenge Your Doubts** – Every time self-doubt creeps in, question it.

◇ **Develop a Winning Track Record** – Set small goals, achieve them, and build momentum.

◇ **Surround Yourself with Strength** – Cut off negativity and align with powerful minds.

◇ **Use Daily Affirmations** – Speak power into your mind: *"I am strong. I am unstoppable. I am built for success."*

◇ **Lion's Exercise:** Write down three past achievements that prove your strength. When self-doubt arises, read them aloud.

Step 3: Developing Mental Resilience – The Art of Bouncing Back

The lion does not give up if it fails a hunt—it **learns, adapts, and strikes again.**

Success is not about avoiding failure; it is about how quickly you recover and keep moving forward.

How to Build Resilience

1. **Accept Failure as Growth**
   - Every setback is an opportunity to learn. **Fail fast, adjust, and attack again.**
2. **Reframe Challenges as Opportunities**
   - Stop seeing difficulties as roadblocks. **They are tests meant to sharpen you.**
3. **Create a 'Bounce-Back' Plan**
   - Instead of dwelling on failures, have a strategy for what to do next.

◇ **Lion's Exercise:** Write down a major setback you've faced. Now, rewrite it as a lesson that made you stronger.

Step 4: Emotional Mastery – Controlling Your Reactions Like a King

A lion does not panic. It does not react emotionally. **It moves with control, purpose, and strategy.**

Many people lose their power because they let their emotions dictate their actions. **You must become the master of your emotions, not a slave to them.**

How to Control Your Emotions Like a Lion

◈ **Pause Before Reacting** – When something triggers you, breathe and think before responding.

◈ **Remove Ego from Decision-Making** – Do not let pride cloud your judgment.

◈ **Practice Stoicism** – Focus on what you can control and ignore what you cannot.

◈ **Turn Negative Energy Into Fuel** – Anger, frustration, and doubt are powerful. Channel them into action.

◈ **Lion's Exercise:** Identify an emotional weakness (e.g., impatience, insecurity). Write one strategy to take control of it starting today.

Step 5: The Power of Relentless Determination

A lion **never** gives up on the hunt. It does not stop because it is tired. It does not hesitate because it has failed before. It pushes forward because **giving up is not an option.**

Success requires the same mindset. **No matter what obstacles arise, you must move forward.**

How to Develop Relentless Determination

◈ **Eliminate the Option of Quitting** – Make failure a lesson, not a stopping point.

◈ **Create Unstoppable Momentum** – Keep taking action, even if progress is slow.

◈ **Stay Connected to Your 'Why'** – Remind yourself daily why you started.

◈ **Adopt a 'Whatever It Takes' Attitude** – Decide that no excuse will stop you.

◈ **Lion's Exercise:** Write down your biggest goal. Then, write: *"I will achieve this no matter what."* Read it daily.

Step 6: Strengthening the Mind and Body for Maximum Power

A lion keeps itself strong. It is **physically powerful and mentally sharp.**

To harness your full strength, you must take care of **both your mind and body.**

How to Keep Yourself at Peak Power

◇ **Mental Strength:**

◇ Read books that sharpen your mind.

◇ Practice meditation to develop control over thoughts.

◇ Engage in problem-solving to keep your mind sharp.

◇ **Physical Strength:**

◇ Exercise regularly to build stamina and resilience.

◇ Eat foods that fuel strength and energy.

◇ Prioritize rest—lions know the value of recovery.

◇ **Lion's Exercise:** Set a weekly goal for both mental and physical training. Track your progress.

Step 7: Aligning with Your Inner Power and Purpose

A lion does not live a life of confusion. It has a **clear purpose**—to rule, to thrive, to lead.

If you are unsure of your purpose, you will always feel lost, weak, and directionless.

How to Align with Your Inner Power

◈ **Ask Yourself: What Do I Want to Be Known For?**

◈ **Visualize the Life You Want and Step Into It**

◈ **Remove Everything That Weakens Your Spirit**

◈ **Operate from Power, Not Fear**

◈ **Lion's Exercise:** Write down **your personal mission statement**—the legacy you want to create.

Conclusion: Becoming the Apex Predator of Your Life

Harnessing inner strength is what separates **leaders from followers, winners from losers, and the dominant from the weak.**

When you master your **beliefs, resilience, emotions, and determination**, nothing will stop you. You will move through life **like a lion—fearless, powerful, and in complete control of your destiny.**

Your Inner Strength Recap:

◈ Develop **unshakable self-belief**—trust your power.

◈ Build **mental resilience**—bounce back from failures instantly.

◈ Master **your emotions**—control your reactions like a king.

◈ Become **relentlessly determined**—never quit, no matter what.

◈ Strengthen **your mind and body**—stay at peak performance.

◈ Align **with your purpose**—move through life with intention and power.

Chapter 6: Surviving and Thriving in Challenges

How to Face Adversity Like a Lion and Come Out Stronger

In the wild, the lion does not live a life of ease. It faces droughts, rival predators, injuries, and fierce battles. Yet, it **does not cower, it does not retreat—it adapts, fights, and dominates.**

Life is the same. Challenges are inevitable. Hardships will come. Obstacles will test your resolve. **But how you respond determines whether you survive or thrive.**

Some people break under pressure, while others **rise through the storm, growing stronger and more unstoppable than ever.** This chapter will teach you how to **embrace challenges, turn adversity into opportunity, and emerge victorious in any situation.**

Step 1: Accepting Challenges as a Part of the Journey

The weak complain about hardship. The lion expects it.

Many people resist challenges, wishing for an easier life. But the truth is **greatness is forged in adversity.** Every struggle is a test designed to sharpen you.

Reframing Challenges as Fuel for Growth

Instead of seeing obstacles as problems, start seeing them as:

◇ **Opportunities to grow stronger** – Every challenge makes you more powerful.

◇ **A test of your resilience** – Will you rise or retreat?

◇ **A sharpening tool** – Hardships refine you into your most powerful self.

◇ **A necessary part of success** – No great leader, athlete, or entrepreneur has avoided struggle.

◇ **Lion's Exercise:** Think of a major challenge you've faced. How did it make you stronger? Write down the lesson it taught you.

Step 2: Developing an Unbreakable Mindset

A lion does not let failure break it. It does not allow setbacks to crush its spirit. **It keeps moving forward.**

To thrive in challenges, you must develop an **unbreakable mental foundation** that prevents you from being defeated by hardship.

How to Build an Indestructible Mindset

1. **Adopt the "No Retreat" Mentality**
   - There is no going back. Once you commit to a goal, **you must push forward.**
2. **Control Your Thoughts**
   - Your mind will try to create doubt. **Reject weak thoughts.** Replace them with power:
     - *"I am built for this."*
     - *"I overcome everything in my path."*
     - *"This challenge will not break me—it will build me."*
3. **Stay Calm Under Pressure**
   - Lions do not panic. **They analyze, adapt, and act.**
   - When faced with stress, breathe, refocus, and strategize instead of reacting emotionally.

◈ **Lion's Exercise:** Write down **three affirmations** that reinforce your inner strength. Repeat them daily.

Step 3: Turning Setbacks into Stepping Stones

Every lion **loses a hunt** at some point. But it does not stop hunting. It **learns, adapts, and tries again.**

Too many people give up after failure, not realizing that **failure is a stepping stone, not a dead end.**

How to Use Setbacks to Your Advantage

◈ **Analyze what went wrong** – What was the lesson? How can you improve?

◈ **Adjust your approach** – Do not repeat the same mistake.

◈ **Stay persistent** – Keep moving forward, no matter how many times you fall.

◈ **Refuse to be emotionally defeated** – Failure only wins if you let it stop you.

◈ **Lion's Exercise:** Write down **one failure** you've had. Now, write down **one action you can take to turn it into a win.**

Step 4: Building Physical and Mental Endurance

A lion does not just survive—it **stays at peak condition.**

Success in challenges requires **both mental and physical resilience.** If you are weak in either, adversity will break you.

How to Strengthen Your Mind and Body to Endure Challenges

Mental Strength:

◈ Read books that sharpen your perspective.

◈ Challenge yourself daily—do something difficult every day.

◈ Meditate or engage in mental clarity exercises.

Physical Strength:

◈ Exercise regularly—strong body, strong mind.

◈ Get proper rest—recovery is part of resilience.

◈ Fuel yourself correctly—eat for energy and focus.

◈ **Lion's Exercise:** Set a goal to **push your limits** this week (mentally or physically). Track your progress.

Step 5: The Power of Adaptability – Shifting Strategy When Needed

Lions do not always hunt the same way. If conditions change, they adapt.

If you are rigid in life, you will **break when things do not go as planned.** But if you develop adaptability, you will survive anything.

How to Stay Adaptable in Challenges

⬦ **Be willing to pivot** – If something isn't working, change tactics.

⬦ **Keep learning** – Stay ahead by gaining new skills and knowledge.

⬦ **Develop multiple strategies** – Always have **a backup plan.**

⬦ **Lion's Exercise:** Think of a time when life forced you to change plans. What did you learn? Write down how you can become more adaptable in the future.

Step 6: Building a Warrior's Mindset – Handling Pressure Like a Champion

The lion does not collapse under pressure. It **performs at its best when the stakes are high.**

Life's greatest rewards come when you are able to **handle pressure without breaking down.**

How to Stay Strong Under Pressure

⬦ **Breathe and focus on the present moment** – Do not let emotions take over.

⬦ **Make logical, not emotional, decisions** – Stay strategic.

⬦ **Trust yourself** – Confidence in your abilities keeps you steady.

⬦ **Remember: Every challenge is temporary** – Keep moving forward.

⬦ **Lion's Exercise:** Identify **one high-pressure situation** you struggle with. Write down three ways you can handle it better next time.

Step 7: Surrounding Yourself with Strength

A lion does not survive alone. It moves with a **strong, loyal pride.**

The people you surround yourself with will determine whether you thrive or crumble in challenges.

How to Build a Strong Support System

◈ **Eliminate negative, weak-minded influences** – They drain your energy.

◈ **Find people who push you forward** – Strong minds sharpen each other.

◈ **Seek mentors or role models** – Learn from those who have already overcome obstacles.

◈ **Lion's Exercise:** List **three people** in your life who strengthen you. Now, list **three who weaken you.** Make adjustments accordingly.

Step 8: The Never-Back-Down Mentality – Winning No Matter What

A lion does not quit the hunt. It does not surrender its throne. It keeps fighting **until it wins.**

This is the mentality of champions. **No matter what happens, you keep moving forward.**

How to Develop a 'Never-Back-Down' Attitude

◈ **Decide that quitting is not an option** – Make it non-negotiable.

◈ **Accept that struggle is part of success** – Nothing worthwhile is easy.

◈ **Remind yourself why you started** – Stay connected to your mission.

◈ **Push through the pain** – Success is on the other side of hardship.

◈ **Lion's Exercise:** Write down **your personal declaration of strength**—a promise that you will never back down from your goals. Read it daily.

Conclusion: Dominating Every Challenge in Life

Life will test you. It will try to break you. But if you are **mentally, physically, and emotionally prepared, nothing will stop you.**

A lion is not the king because it avoids struggle—it is the king because it **overcomes every battle.**

Your Survival and Thriving Recap:

◈ Accept **challenges as opportunities, not roadblocks.**

◈ Build **an unbreakable mindset**—you do not fold under pressure.

◈ Turn **setbacks into stepping stones.**

◈ Strengthen **your mind and body** to endure anything.

◈ Develop **adaptability**—adjust when needed.

◈ Surround yourself with **strong, powerful people.**

◈ Adopt the **Never-Back-Down** mentality—no excuses, no quitting.

Chapter 7: Sustaining Long-Term Success
How to Stay at the Top and Continue Thriving Like a Lion

Reaching success is one thing. **Sustaining it is another.**

Many rise to the top only to **fall just as fast** because they lack the discipline, vision, or adaptability to maintain their success. A lion does not just hunt once and survive—it **repeats the process daily, refining its skills, marking its territory, and ensuring its dominance over time.**

Success is **not** a one-time event—it is a **way of life.** This chapter will teach you how to **stay at the top, grow continuously, and ensure that you never lose momentum.**

Step 1: Developing a Long-Term Vision – Thinking Like a King

A lion does not live in the moment alone—it **rules with a long-term strategy.**

Many people achieve success and then **lose focus, become complacent, or fail to plan for the future.** If you want to sustain success, you must always be thinking **years ahead, not just days or months.**

How to Create a Long-Term Vision

◈ **Define what long-term success looks like for you** – Is it financial freedom? Legacy? Influence? Growth?

◈ **Break it down into milestones** – Success is maintained by continuous small wins over time.

◈ **Adapt and evolve** – If conditions change, so must your approach.

◈ **Think beyond yourself** – How will your success impact others, your industry, and future generations?

◈ **Lion's Exercise:** Write down where you want to be **in 5 years.** What will success look like for you at that point?

Step 2: Avoiding Complacency – Staying Hungry Like a Lion

A lion does not stop hunting after one meal. It **stays hungry.**

Many people become **too comfortable** after achieving success. They slow down, get distracted, or stop pushing forward. **This is why most people never maintain long-term dominance.**

How to Stay Hungry for Success

◈ **Set new challenges regularly** – Never allow yourself to plateau.

◈ **Surround yourself with bigger thinkers** – Being the smartest in the room is dangerous.

◈ **Keep learning and evolving** – New knowledge keeps you sharp and adaptable.

◈ **Avoid comfort zones** – Growth happens when you stay challenged.

◈ **Lion's Exercise:** What is one **new challenge** you can set for yourself today to ensure you keep growing?

Step 3: Mastering Adaptability – Staying Ahead of the Competition

The savannah is always changing—new threats arise, prey moves, seasons shift. The **lion survives because it adapts.**

If you want long-term success, you must be **flexible, innovative, and ahead of the curve.** The moment you resist change, you begin to decline.

How to Stay Adaptable and Ahead

◈ **Study trends and anticipate shifts** – Never be caught off guard by change.

◈ **Innovate constantly** – Keep improving your methods, products, and strategies.

◈ **Be willing to reinvent yourself** – Growth requires transformation.

◈ **Learn from competition** – Watch how others evolve and refine your own approach.

◈ **Lion's Exercise:** Identify **one area of your life or business** where you need to adapt to stay ahead. Make a plan to shift your approach.

Step 4: Strengthening Your Mental and Physical Power

A lion that weakens is a lion that becomes vulnerable. Strength is not a **one-time achievement**—it is **a lifelong commitment.**

Success is maintained by **keeping your mind sharp and your body strong**. The moment you neglect either, you start losing your edge.

How to Maintain Mental and Physical Strength

◇ **Mental Strength:**

◇ Keep reading, learning, and expanding your knowledge.

◇ Engage in deep thinking and self-reflection.

◇ Stay disciplined in daily habits.

◇ **Physical Strength:**

◇ Maintain a consistent fitness routine.

◇ Eat for energy and endurance.

◇ Prioritize sleep and recovery.

◇ **Lion's Exercise:** Write down one new habit to strengthen your **mind** and one to strengthen your **body** starting today.

Step 5: Building and Protecting Your Legacy

A lion is remembered **not just for its strength but for the impact it leaves.**

Your success should not be **temporary**—it should create a legacy that lasts. The greatest leaders, entrepreneurs, and visionaries **do not just succeed for themselves—they create something bigger than them.**

How to Build a Lasting Legacy

◇ **Share knowledge** – Teach others what you have learned.

◇ **Create something bigger than yourself** – A brand, a movement, an impact.

◇ **Make strategic moves for the future** – Long-term success requires forward-thinking decisions.

◇ **Ensure your success outlives you** – What will people remember you for?

◇ **Lion's Exercise:** Write down what you want your **legacy** to be. How will your success continue even after you are gone?

Step 6: Keeping Your Circle Strong – Surrounding Yourself with Power

A lion does not rule alone—it thrives because of its **pride**.

Long-term success is not just about personal effort—it is about **who you surround yourself with.** The wrong people can bring you down just as fast as the right ones can elevate you.

How to Build and Maintain a Powerful Circle

◈ **Eliminate weak-minded influences** – Remove negativity from your environment.

◈ **Network with ambitious and successful individuals** – Surround yourself with people who inspire you.

◈ **Keep mentors and advisors** – Learn from those who have sustained success.

◈ **Build strong partnerships** – Success is easier when you collaborate with the right people.

◈ **Lion's Exercise:** Identify three people who **elevate** you and three who **hold you back.** Make adjustments accordingly.

Step 7: Maintaining Financial Stability and Growth

Many people achieve financial success only to **lose it due to poor management.**

A lion does not waste its energy—it **maximizes every opportunity.** In the same way, you must protect and grow your financial success wisely.

How to Maintain and Expand Wealth

◈ **Invest in assets, not liabilities** – Focus on long-term financial stability.

◈ **Save and reinvest wisely** – Money should work for you, not disappear.

◈ **Avoid reckless spending** – Financial discipline ensures sustainability.

◈ **Diversify income streams** – Do not depend on just one source of success.

◈ **Lion's Exercise:** Write down three ways you can **grow and protect** your wealth over the next five years.

Step 8: Staying Consistent – The Key to Lifelong Success

A lion does not hunt only when it feels like it. **It remains consistent.**

Many people start strong but fail because they **lack consistency**. Long-term success is built through **small, disciplined actions repeated daily.**

How to Maintain Relentless Consistency

◇ **Create daily success rituals** – Structure your habits for maximum results.

◇ **Track progress** – Regularly review where you are and adjust as needed.

◇ **Stay committed through ups and downs** – Never lose sight of the bigger picture.

◇ **Keep momentum alive** – Small actions daily lead to massive success over time.

◇ **Lion's Exercise:** Write down three things you will commit to **doing daily** to ensure continued success.

Conclusion: The Path to Lifelong Greatness

Success is not a sprint—it is a **lifelong hunt.**

The weak rise and fall. **The strong dominate and sustain.**

By following the principles in this chapter, you will not only reach the top—you will **stay there, grow, and leave a lasting impact.**

Your Long-Term Success Recap:

◇ Define a **long-term vision** and work toward it daily.

◇ Stay **hungry** and avoid complacency.

◇ Adapt and evolve with changing circumstances.

◇ Maintain **mental and physical strength** to stay at peak performance.

◇ Build a **legacy that lasts beyond you.**

◇ Surround yourself with **powerful, ambitious people.**

◇ Manage **wealth wisely** to sustain financial success.

◇ Stay **consistent**—success is built over time.

Chapter 8: Command Respect, Influence, and Authority in Your Domain

How to Establish Yourself as an Unquestioned Leader and Apex Predator in Your Field

A lion does not demand respect—it **commands it** by its very presence.

It does not beg for influence—it **naturally exerts it** through its dominance, confidence, and undeniable strength.

It does not ask for authority—it **takes it** by proving, time and time again, that it is the true ruler of its domain.

In the modern world, success is not enough. **You must establish yourself as a leader, someone others look up to, follow, and respect.** Whether in business, personal life, or any field of expertise, **commanding respect, influence, and authority** ensures that you remain at the top of the hierarchy, controlling opportunities, dictating terms, and shaping the future on your terms.

This final chapter will teach you how to **move like a lion—powerful, respected, and unchallenged in your domain.**

Step 1: Establishing Unshakable Confidence – Walking Like a King

A lion does not hesitate. It does not second-guess itself. It moves with **certainty and conviction**, and the world responds accordingly.

If you do not believe in yourself, no one else will. People respect those who **carry themselves with power**—those who are sure of who they are, where they are going, and what they stand for.

How to Build an Aura of Unshakable Confidence

◇ **Master Your Presence** – Stand tall, speak with certainty, and maintain strong eye contact.

◇ **Refuse to Seek Validation** – Lions do not need approval. **Trust yourself fully.**

◇ **Eliminate Weak Language** – Avoid "I think," "I hope," or "maybe." Speak with clarity and conviction.

◇ **Own Every Room You Enter** – When you walk in, **own the space.** Command attention without even speaking.

◇ **Lion's Exercise:** For the next week, practice walking, speaking, and acting **like an apex predator**—with **unshakable confidence.**

Step 2: Demonstrating Mastery – Becoming an Authority in Your Field

A lion commands respect because **it is the best at what it does.**

The most respected individuals in any domain are **masters** of their craft. Whether you are an entrepreneur, an artist, an athlete, or a thought leader, your influence grows **when people recognize your expertise and results.**

How to Establish Yourself as an Authority

◈ **Master Your Skillset** – Never stop improving. Be **so good they can't ignore you.**

◈ **Share Valuable Knowledge** – Teach, write, or speak on your expertise. Become **a thought leader.**

◈ **Let Results Speak for You** – Show undeniable proof of your ability (success stories, achievements, case studies).

◈ **Control the Narrative** – Position yourself as **the go-to person** in your industry or field.

◈ **Lion's Exercise:** Identify one area where you can **increase your mastery** and one way you can **showcase your expertise to the world.**

Step 3: The Art of Influence – Leading Without Force

A lion does not force others to follow—it moves with power, and others **naturally fall in line.**

Influence is **not** about control—it is about **inspiration, respect, and value.** If people see you as valuable, they will want to follow, support, and promote you.

How to Cultivate Magnetic Influence

◈ **Be Consistent in Your Message** – People trust those who are **clear in their vision.**

◈ **Provide Value First** – The more you give, the more people listen to you.

◈ **Stay Relatable** – People follow those they connect with. Show **authenticity** and **realness.**

◈ **Master the Art of Storytelling** – Stories create deep influence. Share **your journey, struggles, and victories.**

◈ **Lion's Exercise:** Identify **one way** you can start influencing others today—whether through content, mentorship, or leadership.

Step 4: Commanding Respect – The Laws of Power
Respect is **not given—it is earned and maintained.**
If you do not enforce your position, others will challenge it. **If you do not set boundaries, people will disrespect them.**

How to Command Respect Like a King
◇ **Set Clear Boundaries** – Let people know what is and is not acceptable. **Do not tolerate disrespect.**
◇ **Be Selective with Your Time and Energy** – Not everyone deserves your attention.
◇ **Hold Yourself to a Higher Standard** – Lead by example.
◇ **Refuse to Overexplain Yourself** – Lions do not justify their actions—they act with conviction.
◇ **Lion's Exercise:** Identify one area of your life where you need to **set stronger boundaries** and implement a change immediately.

Step 5: Building a Loyal Following – Creating a Pride That Backs You

A lion's strength is amplified by its **pride—a strong, loyal group that moves with it.**

Your power and success will multiply when you **surround yourself with the right people**—those who respect, support, and elevate you.

How to Build a Strong and Loyal Network

◇ **Identify Your Inner Circle** – Who are your true allies? Strengthen those bonds.

◇ **Mentor and Elevate Others** – When you help others succeed, you gain lasting loyalty.

◇ **Cultivate a Strong Reputation** – Be known for **integrity, reliability, and wisdom.**

◇ **Eliminate the Disloyal and Weak-Minded** – Not everyone deserves access to you.

◇ **Lion's Exercise:** List **three people who uplift you** and **three people who drain you.** Adjust your inner circle accordingly.

Step 6: Expanding Your Territory – Dominating New Domains

A lion does not rule just one small part of the land—it **expands its territory, ensuring it remains in control.**

Once you establish yourself, the next step is **growth—expanding your reach, impact, and influence into new areas.**

How to Expand and Scale Your Influence

◈ **Seek New Opportunities** – Look beyond your current field for ways to expand.

◈ **Collaborate with Other Powerful Individuals** – Partner with those who can elevate you.

◈ **Establish Multiple Revenue Streams** – Financial dominance increases your ability to lead.

◈ **Create a Lasting Brand or Movement** – Leave something behind that continues to grow.

◈ **Lion's Exercise:** Write down one way you can **expand your influence or success** beyond your current domain.

Step 7: Leaving a Lasting Impact – Becoming a Legend

True leaders **do not just live—they create legacies that last beyond their lifetime.**

When your name **carries weight even when you're not present**, you have reached the ultimate level of respect, influence, and authority.

How to Create a Legacy That Lives On

◈ **Pass on knowledge and wisdom** – Teach, write, or mentor the next generation.

◈ **Build something permanent** – A business, book, foundation, or movement that carries your name.

◈ **Be remembered for impact, not just success** – Influence **how people think and live.**

◈ **Ensure your values are carried forward** – Make sure your message continues after you.

◈ **Lion's Exercise:** Write down what you want to be **remembered for.** What is your legacy?

Conclusion: You Are the Apex Predator – Own Your Throne

You are no longer just a player in the game—you are **the ruler of your domain.**

You **command respect.**

You **influence minds.**

You **hold authority in your field.**

You **move with power, wisdom, and strategy.**

This is your final transformation. You are no longer simply surviving—you are **dominating, expanding, and thriving at the highest level.**

Your Final Recap:

◈ Move with **unshakable confidence**—own every space you enter.

◈ Demonstrate **mastery**—be the best at what you do.

◈ Cultivate **influence**—lead through inspiration and power.

◈ Command **respect**—set strong boundaries and standards.

◈ Build a **loyal following**—surround yourself with strength.

◈ Expand your **territory**—grow into new opportunities.

◈ Leave a **lasting legacy**—make your impact eternal.

◈ **This is it. Your throne is waiting. Step forward and rule.**

Appendix A: Tools for Sustained Success
Essential Strategies, Systems, and Resources to Maintain Long-Term Growth and Domination

Success is not just about talent or luck—it is built on **systems, habits, and tools that sustain momentum** over the long run.

A lion does not rely on chance for survival—it has honed instincts, strategies, and techniques that ensure it remains the king of the jungle.

In the same way, **you need a structured system to keep growing, adapting, and thriving in every area of life.** This appendix provides a **comprehensive toolkit** of strategies, mindsets, and resources to help you maintain dominance, avoid burnout, and scale your success to greater heights.

Section 1: The Success Rituals – Daily and Weekly Habits to Stay Sharp

Greatness is not built in a day—it is built through **consistent actions repeated over time.**

To sustain long-term success, you must have **rituals that keep you focused, productive, and mentally sharp.**

Daily Rituals for Peak Performance

◈ **Morning Power Ritual (30-60 Minutes)** – Prime your mind and body for success:

- **Meditation or Visualization (5-10 mins)** – See yourself achieving your goals.
- **Physical Exercise (20-30 mins)** – Keep your body strong and energetic.
- **Affirmations and Intentions (5 mins)** – Reinforce success-driven thoughts.
- **Priority Setting (5 mins)** – Define your top 3 priorities for the day.

⬥ **Nightly Reflection Ritual (15-30 Minutes)** – End the day with purpose:

- **Review Your Progress** – What did you accomplish? What needs improvement?
- **Express Gratitude** – List three things you are grateful for.
- **Plan Tomorrow's Key Actions** – Set yourself up for another productive day.

Weekly Rituals for Long-Term Growth

⬥ **Deep Work Blocks (2-4 Hours Weekly)** – Uninterrupted focus on **high-value** projects.

⬥ **Self-Improvement Session (1 Hour Weekly)** – Read books, take courses, sharpen skills.

⬥ **Networking and Relationship Building (1 Hour Weekly)** – Connect with high-value people.

⬥ **Financial Review (30 Minutes Weekly)** – Track income, expenses, and investments.

⬥ **Physical Challenge (1-2 Hours Weekly)** – Push your body beyond its comfort zone.

⬥ **Success Tool:** Use a **planner or app** (Notion, Trello, Evernote) to track and schedule these rituals.

Section 2: Mindset Strategies for Sustained Growth

Your success is only as strong as your **mindset.**

To ensure you stay at the top, you must continuously reinforce a **powerful, disciplined, and growth-oriented way of thinking.**

Key Mindset Tools for Sustained Success

◈ **The "Next Level" Mentality** – Never stay satisfied with where you are. Always ask: *"What's the next level for me?"*

◈ **Extreme Ownership** – Take full responsibility for everything in your life. No excuses.

◈ **Adaptability Thinking** – View every challenge as an opportunity to grow and evolve.

◈ **Unshakable Self-Belief** – Train your mind to believe: *"I am built for this."*

◈ **Growth Over Comfort** – Seek difficult challenges rather than avoiding them.

◈ **Success Tool:** Keep a **Success Journal** where you write daily victories, lessons learned, and next steps for growth.

Section 3: Systems for Productivity and Time Mastery

Success does not come from **working harder**—it comes from **working smarter** and maximizing every hour of your day.

Time Management Strategies for High Achievers

◈ **The 80/20 Rule (Pareto Principle)** – Identify the **20% of activities that bring 80% of results.** Focus on those.

◈ **The Time Blocking Method** – Set **specific hours** for deep work, meetings, learning, and self-care.

◈ **The "One Thing" Rule** – Each day, focus on **one major task** that moves you closer to your goal.

◈ **Eliminate Low-Value Tasks** – If it doesn't contribute to success, delegate or remove it.

◈ **Success Tool:** Use **time-tracking apps** (RescueTime, Toggl, Clockify) to analyze how you spend your hours.

Section 4: Financial Mastery – Securing Long-Term Wealth and Freedom

A lion does not just hunt for today—it secures its territory for the future.

If you want long-term success, **financial discipline and wealth-building must be a priority.**

Money Management Rules for Long-Term Success

◇ **Live Below Your Means** – Avoid lifestyle inflation.

◇ **Invest Early and Wisely** – Put money into assets that grow over time.

◇ **Diversify Income Streams** – Have multiple sources of revenue to ensure stability.

◇ **Automate Finances** – Set up automatic savings, investments, and expense tracking.

◇ **Track Every Dollar** – Know where your money goes each month.

◇ **Success Tool:** Use finance apps like **YNAB, Mint, or Personal Capital** to monitor and grow your wealth.

Section 5: Relationship and Network Power – Who You Surround Yourself With

A lion's strength is not just in itself—it is in the **pride** it moves with.

To stay successful, you must **align yourself with powerful, ambitious, and growth-oriented individuals.**

How to Build and Maintain a Powerful Network

◈ **Eliminate Weak-Minded People** – Remove negative, lazy, or toxic influences.

◈ **Connect with High-Level Thinkers** – Attend events, mastermind groups, and network with winners.

◈ **Find Mentors and Advisors** – Learn from people who are ahead of you.

◈ **Build a Team** – Whether in business or life, surround yourself with individuals who complement your strengths.

◈ **Success Tool:** Create a **Relationship Audit List** to assess who adds value to your life and who drains your energy.

Section 6: Health, Energy, and Longevity – The Foundation of Sustained Success

A lion cannot rule if it is weak, sick, or exhausted.

To **maintain peak performance**, your health must be a top priority.

Key Habits for Maximum Energy and Longevity

◈ **Move Every Day** – Strength training, cardio, stretching—keep your body powerful.

◈ **Prioritize Sleep** – 7-9 hours of high-quality sleep is **non-negotiable** for performance.

◈ **Fuel Your Body Correctly** – Eat foods that optimize focus, strength, and endurance.

◈ **Reduce Stress** – Use breathing exercises, meditation, or journaling to stay mentally strong.

◈ **Success Tool:** Track health metrics using apps like **MyFitnessPal, WHOOP, or Apple Health.**

Section 7: Continuous Learning and Skill Development

A lion that stops learning becomes prey. **You must always be growing, sharpening your skills, and staying ahead.**

How to Stay a Lifelong Learner

◇ **Read One Book a Month** – Focus on self-improvement, business, or mindset books.

◇ **Take Online Courses** – Platforms like Coursera, Udemy, and MasterClass offer high-value knowledge.

◇ **Engage in Deep Work** – Block out distractions and learn a new skill intensely for 60-90 minutes.

◇ **Attend Seminars and Workshops** – Surround yourself with experts in your field.

◇ **Success Tool:** Use an **Idea Notebook** to write down lessons from books, podcasts, and experiences.

Conclusion: The Ultimate Toolkit for Sustained Success

Sustained success is **not** about working harder—it is about **building systems that keep you sharp, disciplined, and in control.**

Your Final Success Toolkit Recap:

◇ **Daily and Weekly Rituals** – Keep your mind, body, and business growing.

◇ **Elite Mindset Strategies** – Think like a lion, dominate like a king.

◇ **Productivity Systems** – Use time wisely and eliminate distractions.

◇ **Financial Mastery** – Grow wealth and protect it for the long term.

◇ **Strong Network** – Surround yourself with powerful allies.

◇ **Health and Longevity** – Stay physically and mentally sharp.

◇ **Continuous Learning** – Never stop evolving.

The tools are in your hands. Now, use them to dominate, sustain, and expand your success.

◇ **You are the apex predator of your life. Now, go rule.**

Message from the Author:

I hope you enjoyed this book, I love astrology and knew there was not a book such as this out on the shelf. I love metaphysical items as well. Please check out my other books:

-Life of Government Benefits

-My life of Hell

-My life with Hydrocephalus

-Red Sky

-World Domination:Woman's rule

-World Domination:Woman's Rule 2: The War

-Life and Banishment of Apophis: book 1

-The Kidney Friendly Diet

-The Ultimate Hemp Cookbook

-Creating a Dispensary(legally)

-Cleanliness throughout life: the importance of showering from childhood to adulthood.

-Strong Roots: The Risks of Overcoddling children

-Hemp Horoscopes: Cosmic Insights and Earthly Healing

- Celestial Hemp Navigating the Zodiac: Through the Green Cosmos

-Astrological Hemp: Aligning The Stars with Earth's Ancient Herb

-The Astrological Guide to Hemp: Stars, Signs, and Sacred Leaves

-Green Growth: Innovative Marketing Strategies for your Hemp Products and Dispensary

-Cosmic Cannabis

-Astrological Munchies

-Henry The Hemp

-Zodiacal Roots: The Astrological Soul Of Hemp

- Green Constellations: Intersection of Hemp and Zodiac

-Hemp in The Houses: An astrological Adventure Through The Cannabis Galaxy

-Galactic Ganja Guide

Heavenly Hemp

Zodiac Leaves

Doctor Who Astrology

Cannastrology

Stellar Satvias and Cosmic Indicas

Celestial Cannabis: A Zodiac Journey

AstroHerbology: The Sky and The Soil: Volume 1

AstroHerbology:Celestial Cannabis:Volume 2

Cosmic Cannabis Cultivation

The Starry Guide to Herbal Harmony: Volume 1

The Starry Guide to Herbal Harmony: Cannabis Universe: Volume 2

Yugioh Astrology: Astrological Guide to Deck, Duels and more

Nightmare Mansion: Echoes of The Abyss

Nightmare Mansion 2: Legacy of Shadows

Nightmare Mansion 3: Shadows of the Forgotten

Nightmare Mansion 4: Echoes of the Damned

The Life and Banishment of Apophis: Book 2

Nightmare Mansion: Halls of Despair

Healing with Herb: Cannabis and Hydrocephalus

Planetary Pot: Aligning with Astrological Herbs: Volume 1

Fast Track to Freedom: 30 Days to Financial Independence Using AI, Assets, and Agile Hustles

Cosmic Hemp Pathways

How to Become Financially Free in 30 Days: 10,000 Paths to Prosperity

Zodiacal Herbage: Astrological Insights: Volume 1

Nightmare Mansion: Whispers in the Walls

The Daleks Invade Atlantis

Henry the hemp and Hydrocephalus

10X The Kidney Friendly Diet

Cannabis Universe: Adult coloring book

Hemp Astrology: The Healing Power of the Stars

Zodiacal Herbage: Astrological Insights: Cannabis Universe: Volume 2

<u>**Planetary Pot: Aligning with Astrological Herbs: Cannabis Universes: Volume 2**</u>

Doctor Who Meets the Replicators and SG-1: The Ultimate Battle for Survival

Nightmare Mansion: Curse of the Blood Moon

<u>**The Celestial Stoner: A Guide to the Zodiac**</u>

Cosmic Pleasures: Sex Toy Astrology for Every Sign

Hydrocephalus Astrology: Navigating the Stars and Healing Waters

Lapis and the Mischievous Chocolate Bar

Celestial Positions: Sexual Astrology for Every Sign

Apophis's Shadow Work Journal: **:** A Journey of Self-Discovery and Healing

Kinky Cosmos: Sexual Kink Astrology for Every Sign

Digital Cosmos: The Astrological Digimon Compendium

Stellar Seeds: The Cosmic Guide to Growing with Astrology

Apophis's Daily Gratitude Journal

Cat Astrology: Feline Mysteries of the Cosmos

The Cosmic Kama Sutra: An Astrological Guide to Sexual Positions

Unleash Your Potential: A Guided Journal Powered by AI Insights

Whispers of the Enchanted Grove

Cosmic Pleasures: An Astrological Guide to Sexual Kinks

369, 12 Manifestation Journal

Whisper of the nocturne journal(blank journal for writing or drawing)

The Boogey Book

Locked In Reflection: A Chastity Journey Through Locktober

Generating Wealth Quickly:

How to Generate $100,000 in 24 Hours

Star Magic: Harness the Power of the Universe

The Flatulence Chronicles: A Fart Journal for Self-Discovery

The Doctor and The Death Moth

Seize the Day: A Personal Seizure Tracking Journal

The Ultimate Boogeyman Safari: A Journey into the Boogie World and Beyond

Whispers of Samhain: 1,000 Spells of Love, Luck, and Lunar Magic: Samhain Spell Book

Apophis's guides:

Witch's Spellbook Crafting Guide for Halloween

<u>Frost & Flame: The Enchanted Yule Grimoire of 1000 Winter Spells</u>

<u>The Ultimate Boogey Goo Guide & Spooky Activities for Halloween Fun</u>

Harmony of the Scales: A Libra's Spellcraft for Balance and Beauty

The Enchanted Advent: 36 Days of Christmas Wonders

Nightmare Mansion: The Labyrinth of Screams

Harvest of Enchantment: 1,000 Spells of Gratitude, Love, and Fortune for Thanksgiving

The Boogey Chronicles: A Journal of Nightly Encounters and Shadowy Secrets

The 12 Days of Financial Freedom: A Step-by-Step Christmas Countdown to Transform Your Finances

Sigil of the Eternal Spiral Blank Journal

A Christmas Feast: Timeless Recipes for Every Meal

Holiday Stress-Free Solutions: A Survival Guide to Thriving During the Festive Season

Yu-Gi-Oh! Holiday Gifting Mastery: The Ultimate Guide for Fans and Newcomers Alike

Holiday Harmony: A Hydrocephalus Survival Guide for the Festive Season

Celestial Craft: The Witch's Almanac for 2025 – A Cosmic Guide to Manifestations, Moons, and Mystical Events

Doctor Who: The Toymaker's Winter Wonderland

Tulsa King Unveiled: A Thrilling Guide to Stallone's Mafia Masterpiece

Pendulum Craft: A Complete Guide to Crafting and Using Personalized Divination Tools

Nightmare Mansion: Santa's Eternal Eve

Starlight Noel: A Cosmic Journey through Christmas Mysteries

The Dark Architect: Unlocking the Blueprint of Existence

Surviving the Embrace: The Ultimate Guide to Encounters with The Hugging Molly

The Enchanted Codex: Secrets of the Craft for Witches, Wiccans, and Pagans

Harvest of Gratitude: A Complete Thanksgiving Guide

Yuletide Essentials: A Complete Guide to an Authentic and Magical Christmas

Celestial Smokes: A Cosmic Guide to Cigars and Astrology

Living in Balance: A Comprehensive Survival Guide to Thriving with Diabetes Insipidus

Cosmic Symbiosis: The Venom Zodiac Chronicles

The Cursed Paw of Ambition

Cosmic Symbiosis: The Astrological Venom Journal

Celestial Wonders Unfold: A Stargazer's Guide to the Cosmos (2024-2029)

The Ultimate Black Friday Prepper's Guide: Mastering Shopping Strategies and Savings

Cosmic Sales: The Astrological Guide to Black Friday Shopping

Legends of the Corn Mother and Other Harvest Myths

Whispers of the Harvest: The Corn Mother's Journal

The Evergreen Spellbook

The Doctor Meets the Boogeyman

The White Witch of Rose Hall's SpellBook

The Gingerbread Golem's Shadow: A Study in Sweet Darkness

The Gingerbread Golem Codex: An Academic Exploration of Sweet Myths

The Gingerbread Golem Grimoire: Sweet Magicks and Spells for the Festive Witch

The Curse of the Gingerbread Golem

10-minute Christmas Crafts for kids

Christmas Crisis Solutions: The Ultimate Last-Minute Survival Guide

Gingerbread Golem Recipes: Holiday Treats with a Magical Twist

The Infinite Key: Unlocking Mystical Secrets of the Ages

Enchanted Yule: A Wiccan and Pagan Guide to a Magical and Memorable Season

Dinosaurs of Power: Unlocking Ancient Magick

Astro-Dinos: The Cosmic Guide to Prehistoric Wisdom

Gallifrey's Yule Logs: A Festive Doctor Who Cookbook

The Dino Grimoire: Secrets of Prehistoric Magick

The Gift They Never Knew They Needed

The Gingerbread Golem's Culinary Alchemy: Enchanting Recipes for a Sweetly Dark Feast

A Time Lord Christmas: Holiday Adventures with the Doctor

Krampusproofing Your Home: Defensive Strategies for Yule

Silent Frights: A Collection of Christmas Creepypastas to Chill Your Bones

Santa Raptor's Jolly Carnage: A Dino-Claus Christmas Tale

Prehistoric Palettes: A Dino Wicca Coloring Journey

The Christmas Wishkeeper Chronicles

The Starlight Sleigh: A Holiday Journey

Elf Secrets: The True Magic of the North Pole

Candy Cane Conjurations

Cooking with Kids: Recipes Under 20 Minutes

Doctor Who: The TARDIS Confiscation

The Anxiety First Aid Kit: Quick Tools to Calm Your Mind

Frosty Whispers: A Winter's Tale

The Infinite Key: Unlocking the Secrets to Prosperity, Resilience, and Purpose

The Grasping Void: Why You'll Regret This Purchase

Astrology for Busy Bees: Star Signs Simplified

The Instant Focus Formula: Cut Through the Noise

The Secret Language of Colors: Unlocking the Emotional Codes

Sacred Fossil Chronicles: Blank Journal

The Christmas Cottage Miracle

Feeding Frenzy: Graboid-Inspired Recipes

Manifest in Minutes: The Quick Law of Attraction Guide

The Symbiote Chronicles: Doctor Who's Venomous Journey

Think Tiny, Grow Big: The Minimalist Mindset

The Energy Key: Unlocking Limitless Motivation

New Year, New Magic: Manifesting Your Best Year Yet

Unstoppable You: Mastering Confidence in Minutes

Infinite Energy: The Secret to Never Feeling Drained

Lightning Focus: Mastering the Art of Productivity in a Distracted World

Saturnalia Manifestation Magick: A Guide to Unlocking Abundance During the Solstice

Graboids and Garland: The Ultimate Tremors-Themed Christmas Guide

12 Nights of Holiday Magic

The Power of Pause: 60-Second Mindfulness Practices

The Quick Reset: How to Reclaim Your Life After Burnout

The Shadow Eater: A Tale of Despair and Survival

The Micro-Mastery Method: Transform Your Skills in Just Minutes a Day

Reclaiming Time: How to Live More by Doing Less

Chronovore: The Eternal Nexus

The Mind Reset: Unlocking Your Inner Peace in a Chaotic World

Confidence Code: Building Unshakable Self-Belief

Baby the Vampire Terrier

Baby the Vampire Terrier's Christmas Adventure

Celestial Streams: The Content Creator's Astrology Manual

The Wealth Whisperer: Unlocking Abundance with Everyday Actions

The Energy Equation: Maximize Your Output Without Burning Out

The Happiness Algorithm: Science-Backed Steps to Joyful Living

Stress-Free Success: Achieving Goals Without Anxiety

Mindful Wealth: The New Blueprint for Financial Freedom

The Festive Flavors of New Year: A Culinary Celebration

The Master's Gambit: Keys of Eternal Power

Shadowed Secrets: Groundhog Day Mysteries

Beneath the Burrow: Lessons from the Groundhog

Spring's Whispers: The Groundhog's Prediction

The Limitless Mindset: Unlock Your Untapped Potential

The Focus Funnel: How to Cut Through Chaos and Get Results

Bold Moves: Building Courage to Live on Your Terms

The Daily Shift: Simple Practices for Lasting Transformation

The Quarter-Life Reset: Thriving in Your 20s and 30s

The Art of Shadowplay: Building Your Own Personal Myth

The Eternal Loop: Finding Purpose in Repetition
Burrowing Wisdom: Life Lessons from the Groundhog
Shadow Work: A Groundhog Day Perspective
Love in Bloom: 5-Minute Romantic Gestures
The Shadowspell Codex: Secrets of Forbidden Magick
The Burnout Cure: Finding Balance in a Busy World
The Groundhog Prophecy: Unlocking Seasonal Secrets
Nog Tales: The Spirited History of Eggnog
Six More Weeks: Embracing Seasonal Transitions
The Lumivian Chronicles: Fragments of the Fifth Dimension
Money on Your Mind: A Beginner's Guide to Wealth
The Focus Fix: Breaking Through Distraction
January's Spirit Keepers: Mystical Protectors of the Cold
Creativity Unchained: Unlocking Your Wildest Ideas in 2025
Manifestation Mastery: 365 Days to Rewrite Your Reality
The Groundhog's Mirror: Reflecting on Change
The Weeping Angels' Christmas Curse
Burrowed in Time: A Groundhog Day Journey
Heartbeats: Poems to Share with Your Valentine
Dino Wicca: The Sacred Grimoire of Prehistoric Magick
Courage of the Pride: Finding Your Inner Roar
The Lion's Leap: Bold Moves for Big Results
Healthy Hustle: Achieving Without Overworking
Practical Manifesting: Turning Dreams into Reality in 2025
Jurassic Pharaohs: Unlocking the Magick of Ancient Egypt
and Dino Wicca
The Happiness Equation: Small Changes for Big Joy
The Confidence Compass: Finding Your Inner Strength
Whispers in the Hollow: Tales of the Forgotten Beasts
Echoes from the Hollow: The Return of Forgotten Beasts
The Hollow Ascendant: The Rise of the Forgotten Beasts
The Relationship Reset: Building Better Connections
Mastering the Morning: How to Win the Day Before 8 AM

The Shadow's Dance: Groundhog Day Symbolism

Cupid's Kitchen: Quick Valentine's Day Recipes

Valentine's Day on a Budget: Love Without Breaking the Bank

Astrocraft: Aligning the Stars in the World of Minecraft

Forecasting Life: Groundhog Day Reflections

Bleeding Hearts: Twisted Tales of Valentine's Terror

Herbal Smoke Revolution: The Ultimate Guide to Nature's Cigarette Alternative

Winter's Wrath: The Complete Survival Blueprint for Extreme Freezes.

The Groundhog's Shadow: A Tale of Seasons

Burrowed Insights: Wisdom from the Groundhog

Sensual Strings: The Art of Erotic Bondage

Whispered Flames: Unlocking the Power of Fire Play

Forgotten Shadows: A Guide to Cryptids Lost to Time

Six Weeks of Secrets: Groundhog Day's Hidden Messages

Shadows and Cycles: Groundhog Day Reflections

The Art of Love Letters: Crafting the Perfect Message

Romantic Getaways at Home: Turning Your Space into Paradise

Purrfect Brews: A Cat Lover's Guide to Coffee and Companionship

The Groundhog's Wisdom: Timeless Lessons for Modern Life

The Shadow Oracle: Groundhog Day as a Predictor

Emerging from the Burrow: A Journey of Renewal

The Language of Love: Learning Your Partner's Love Style

Authorpreneur: The Ultimate Blueprint for Writing, Publishing, and Thriving as an Author

Weathering the Seasons: Groundhog Day Perspectives

Valentine's Day Magic: A Guide to Romantic Rituals

The Shadow Chronicles: Stories of Groundhog Day

Love and Laughter: Fun Games for Valentine's Day

AstroRealty: Unlocking the Stars for Property Success

The Groundhog's Path: A Guide to Seasonal Balance
Groundhog Day Diaries: Reflections in the Shadow
The Groundhog's Light: Illuminating the Path Ahead
Valentine's Traditions from Around the World
AI Wealth Revolution: Unlocking the Trillionaire Mindset
Love Rekindled: Reigniting Passion in Relationships
Single and Thriving: Self-Love on Valentine's Day
Emerald Legends: Mystical Tales of Ireland
Green Alchemy: Harnessing Nature's Magic
The Hearts of Horror: A Valentine's Day Nightmare
The Leprechaun's Guide to Wealth and Wisdom
Dancing with the Sidhe: Celebrating the Otherworld
Shamrocks and Shadows: Mysteries of the Green Isle
Emerald Energy: Harnessing Luck and Growth
The Gingerbread Golem's Valentine: A Sweetheart's Guide to Love and Enchantment
The Celtic Knot: Weaving Life and Destiny
Green Fire: Elemental Magic for St. Patrick's Day
Clover Chronicles: Finding Your Inner Luck
Ireland's Mystical Creatures: A Field Guide
Gingerbread Golem's Love Almanac

If you want solar for your home go here: https://www.harborsolar.live/apophisenterprises/

Get Some Tarot cards: https://www.makeplayingcards.com/sell/apophis-occult-shop

Get some shirts: https://www.bonfire.com/store/apophis-shirt-emporium/

Instagrams:
@apophis_enterprises,
@apophisbookemporium,
@apophisscardshop
Twitter: @apophisenterpr1
Tiktok:@apophisenterprise
Youtube: @sg1fan23477, @FiresideRetreatKingdom
Hive: @sg1fan23477
CheeLee: @SG1fan23477

Podcast: Apophis Chat Zone: https://open.spotify.com/show/5zXbrCLEV2xzCp8ybrfHsk?si=fb4d4fdbdce44dec

Newsletter: https://apophiss-newsletter-27c897.beehiiv.com/

If you want to support me or see posts of other projects that I have come over to: **buymeacoffee.com/mpetchinskg**

I post there daily several times a day

Get your Dinowicca or Christmas themed digital products, especially Santa Raptor songs and other musics. Here: **https://sg1fan23477.gumroad.com**

Apophis Yuletide Digital has not only digital Christmas items, but it will have all things with Dinowicca as well as other Digital products.

www.ingramcontent.com/pod-product-compliance
Ingram Content Group UK Ltd.
Pitfield, Milton Keynes, MK11 3LW, UK
UKHW050552160225
455059UK00017B/366